Reigan's
Bug Book

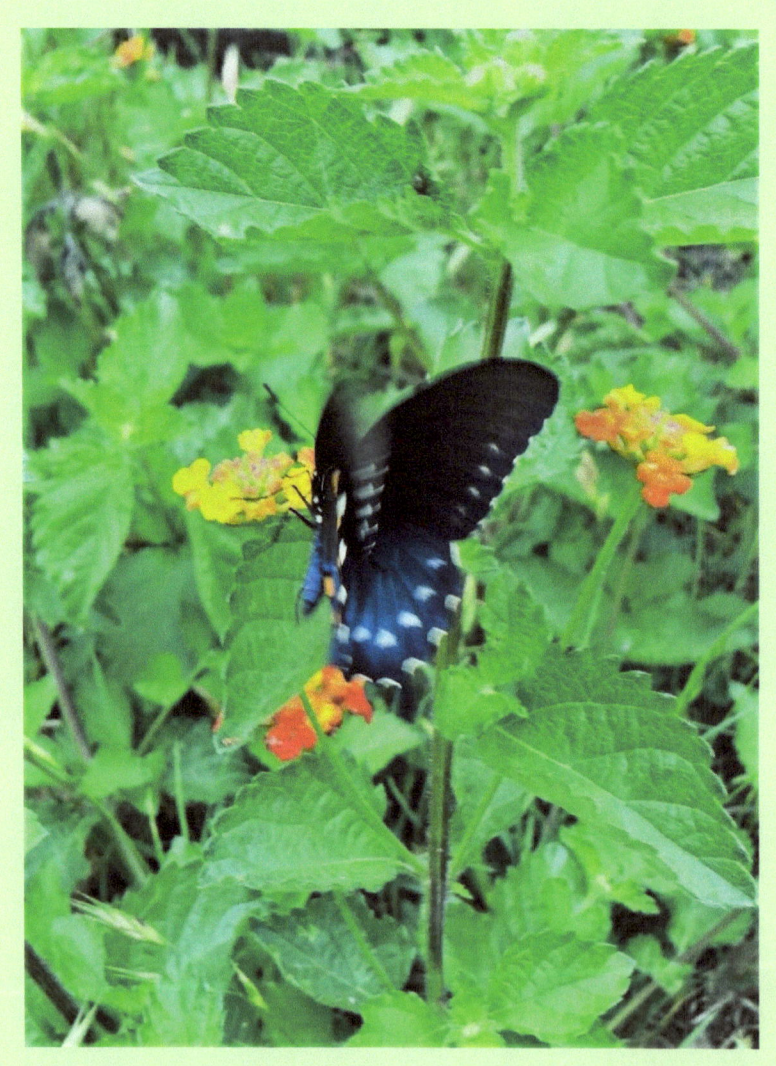

Red Spotted Purple Admiral

The Grandpa Butterfly. Not sure why its call red spotted purple admiral; I haven't seen any red spots or purple on it. This is the butterfly that followed me to work on April 27, 2017.

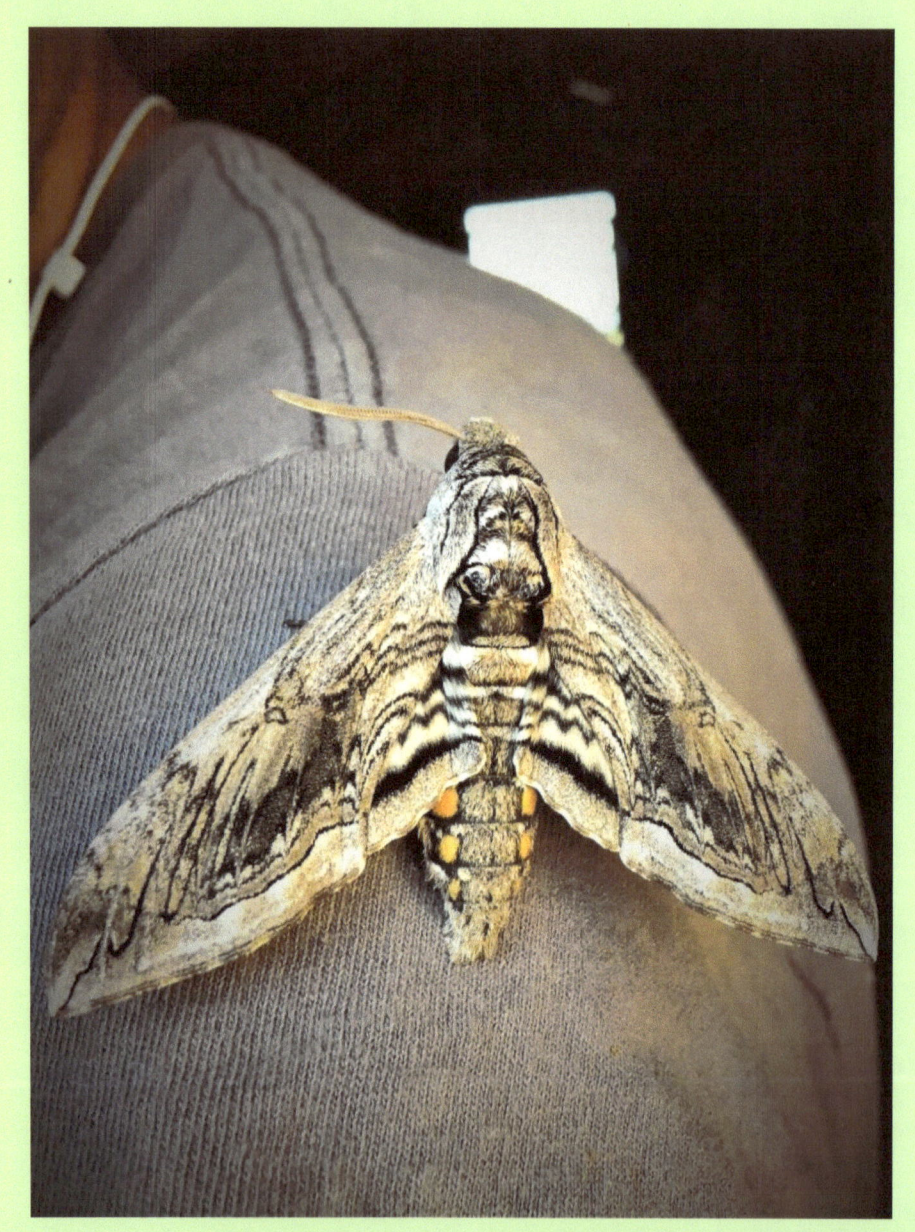

Tomato Hornworm Moth

They have 4-6 inch wing spans. Primary pollinator of the agave plant which gives us tequila. They make a high squeaking noise when startled.

Iconic in the movie Silence of the Lambs.

This guy crawled all over Mike while doing chores at the barn.

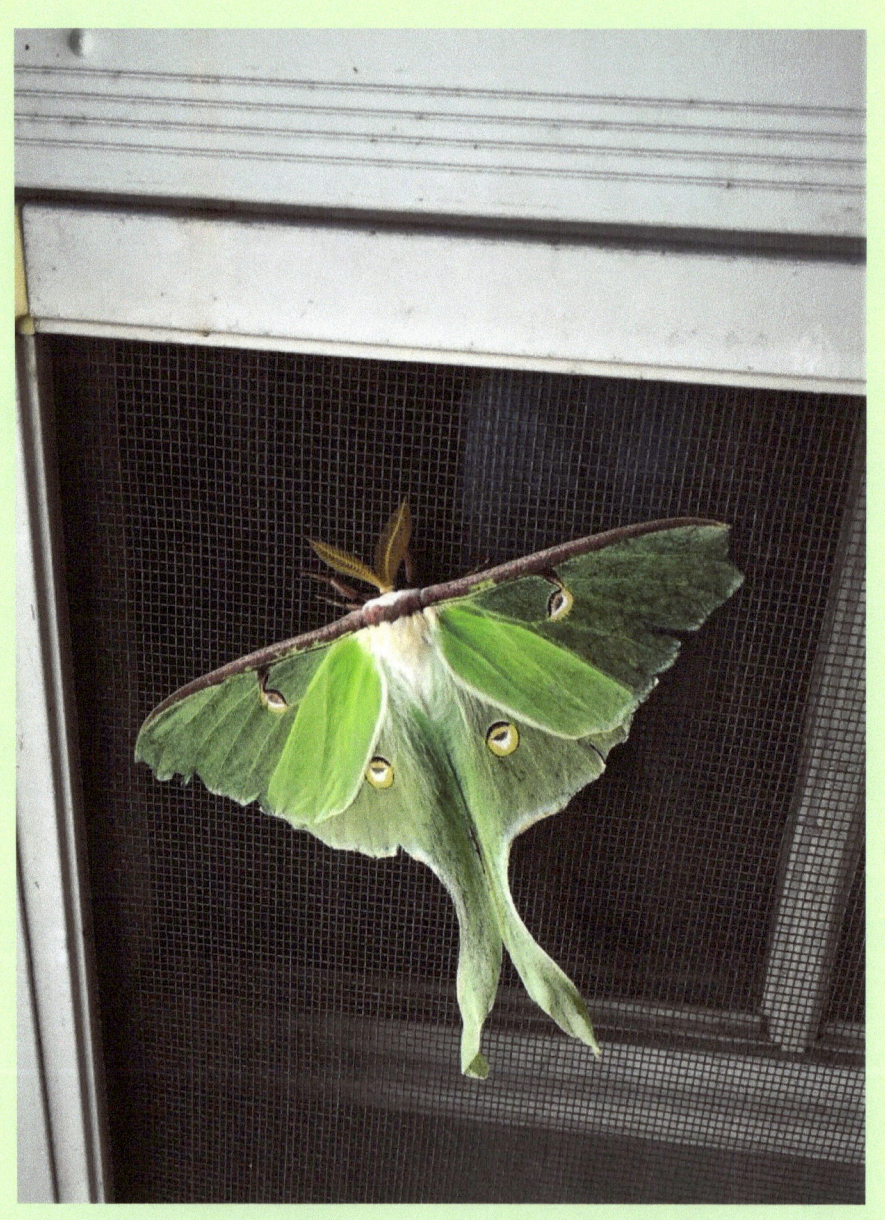

Luna Moth

Only found in North America, it was first reported in literature in the 1700's.

Its wingspan can be up to 4and 1/ inches – the same length as an iPhone 6.

As a moth it has no mouth and no digestive system. It only lives 1 week after coming out of cocoon.

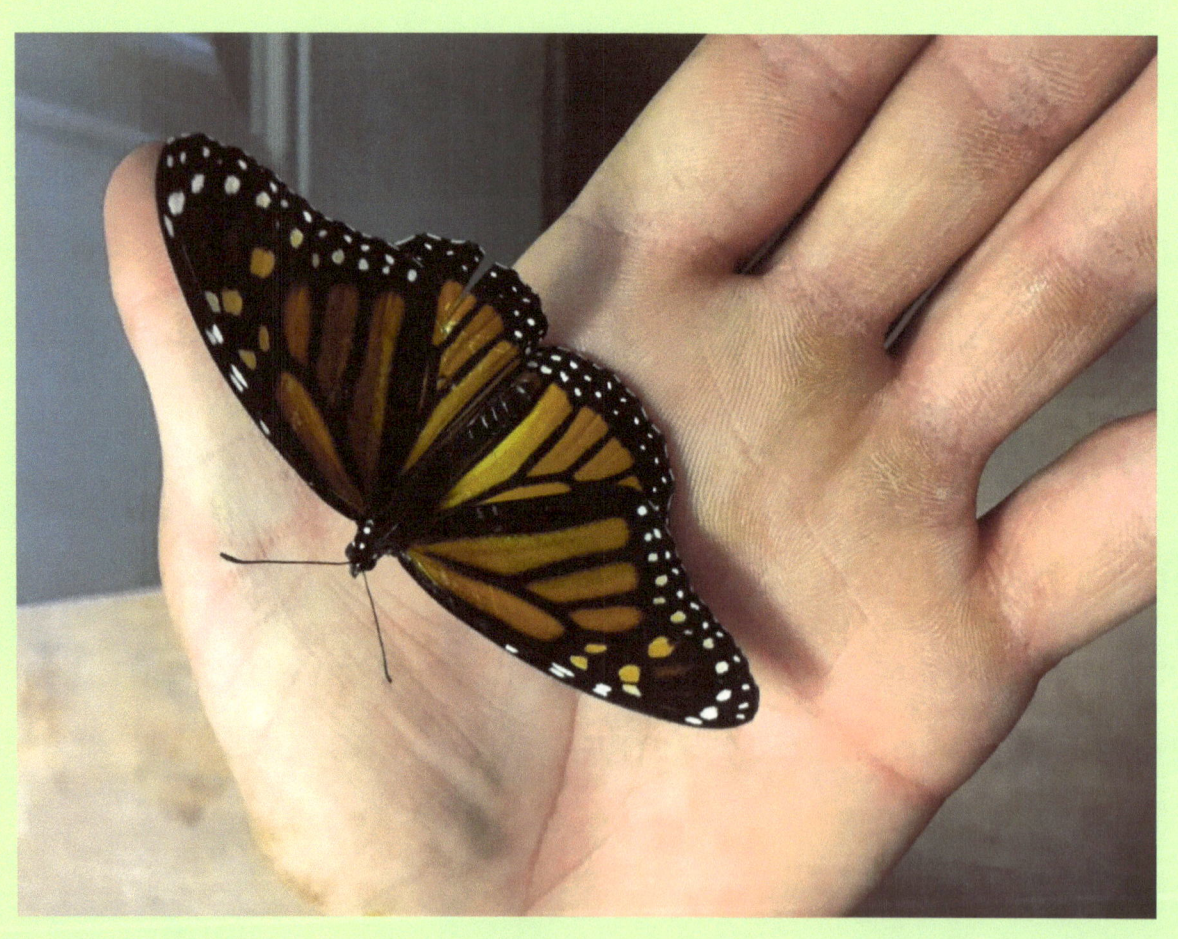

Monarch Butterfly

The king of the butterflies. They go through 4 generations in one year.

Mike found him in the bunk house of the Barn and brought him in to show me. It's a big one.

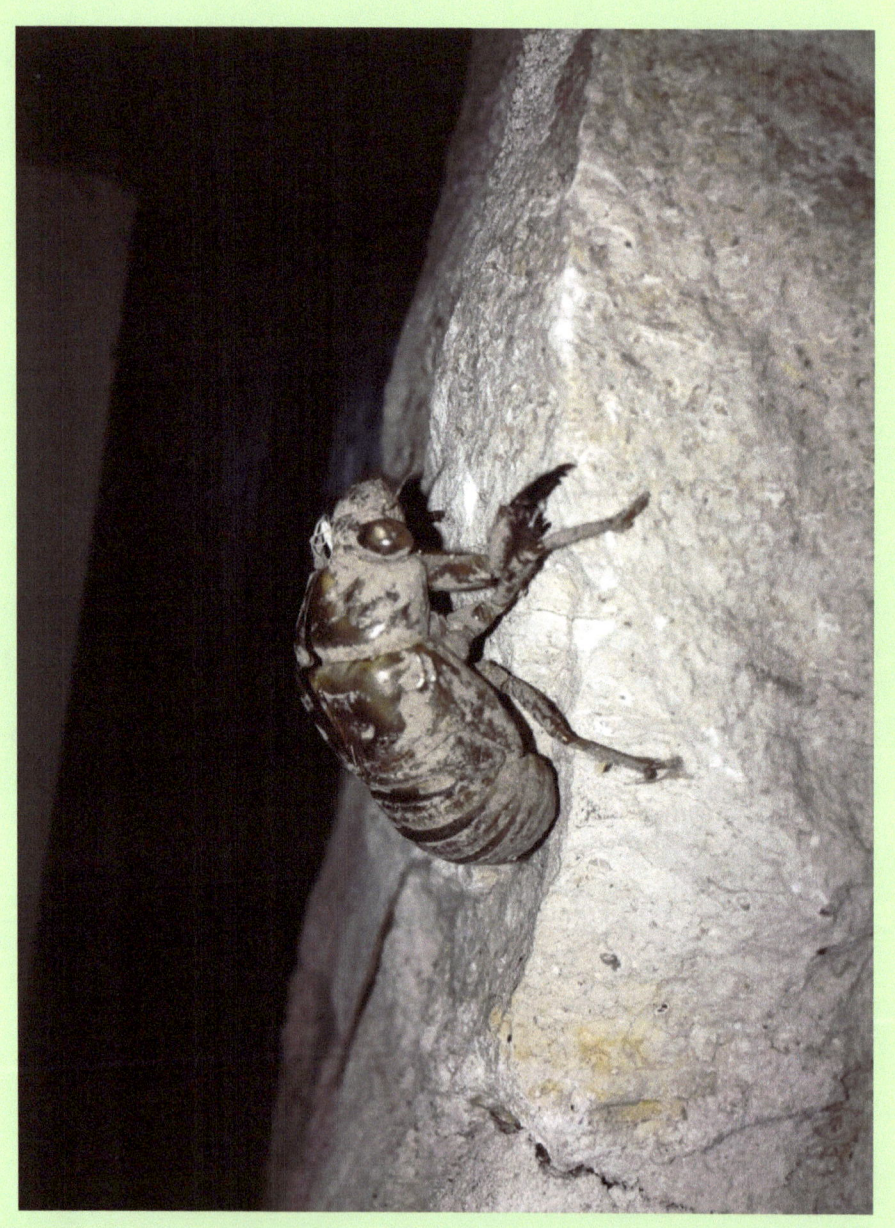

Cicada Shell

Look for them to emerge in New York in 2018. Have fun with them. They make lots of noise and swarm in big numbers.

This shell was found outside the door to the house this spring.

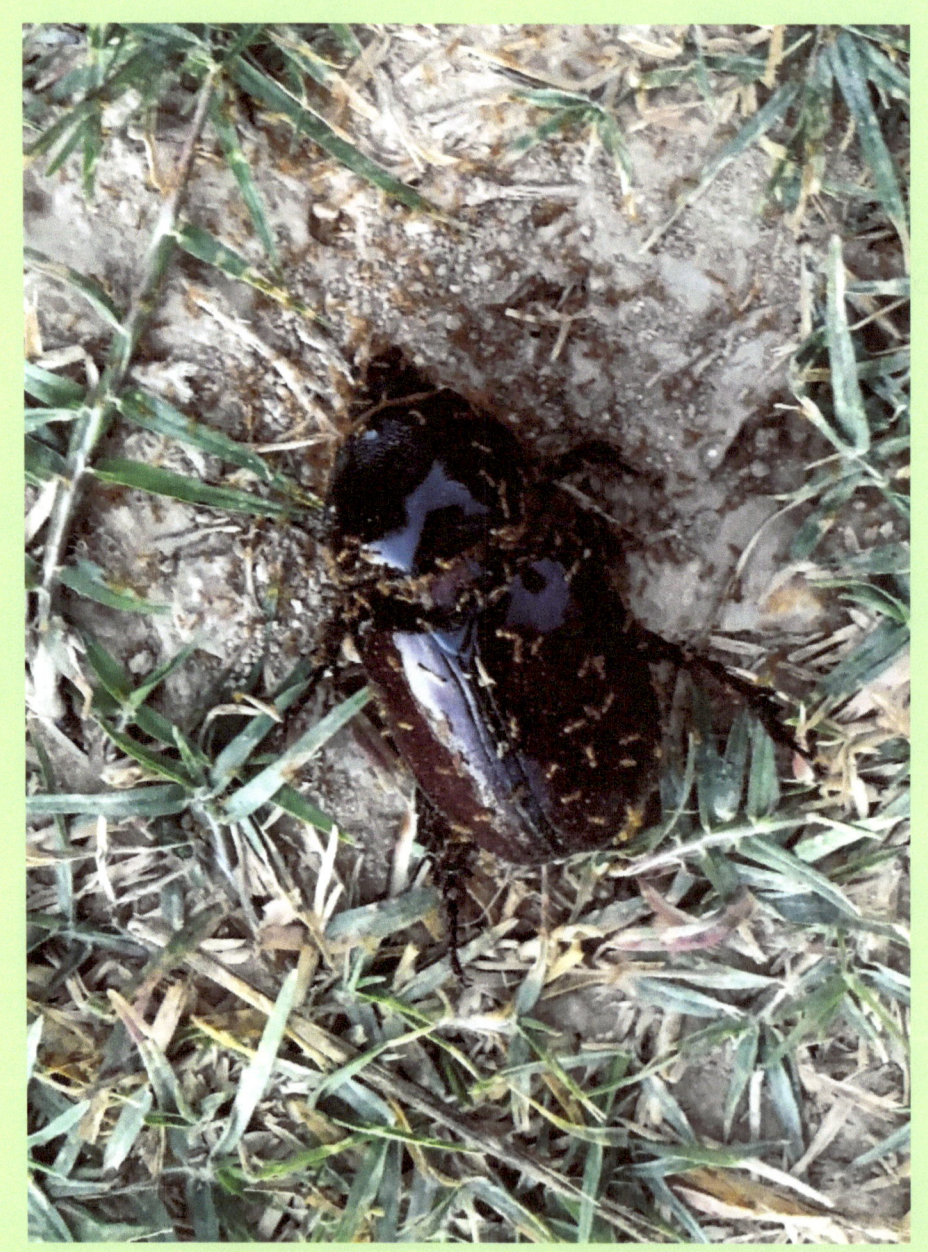

Red ants eating a Beetle.

The cycle of life. Those little red ants are strong and they bite.

I have to be careful because they leave bites worse than a mosquito because they burn and itch.

Poor beetle.

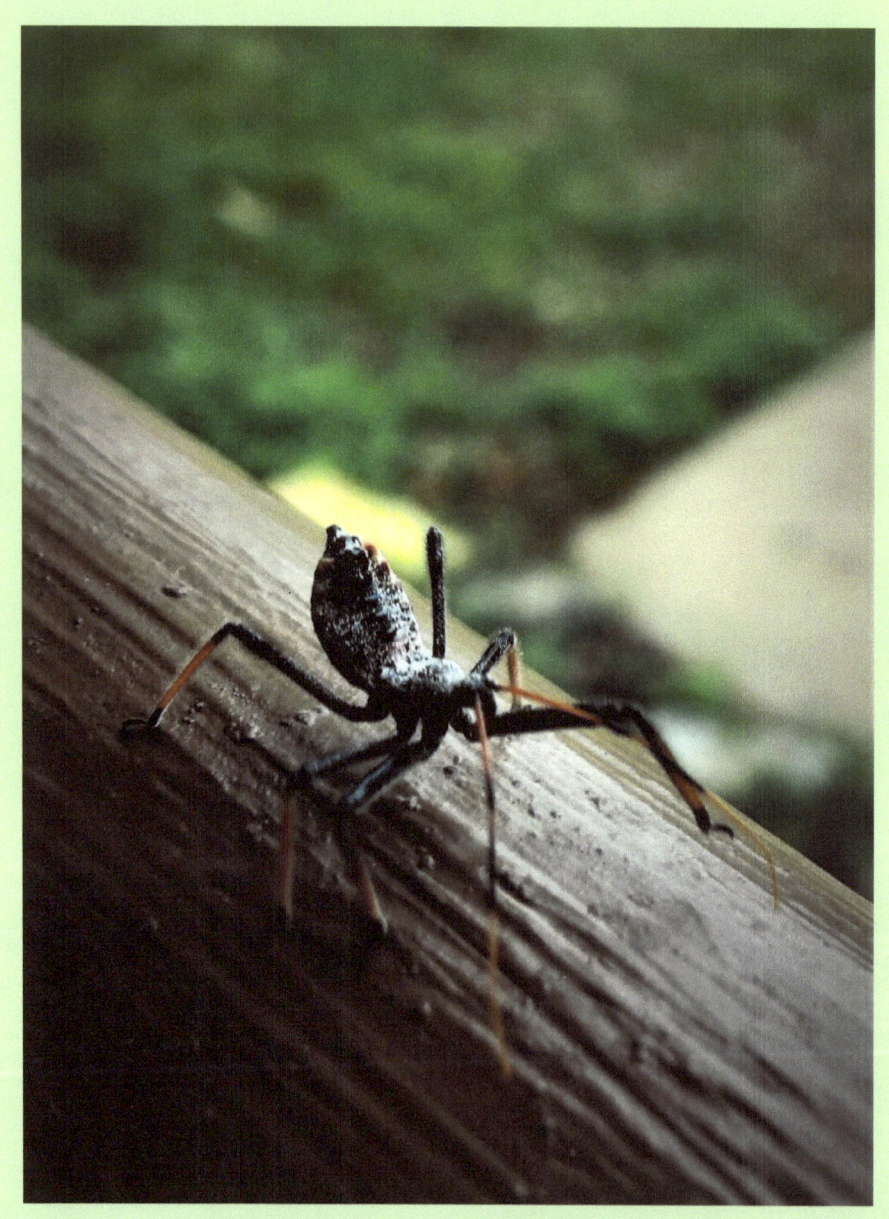

Assassin bug Larva – Wheel bug nymph

They are good for the garden and eat lots of the bad bugs that eat the vegetables. But go in the DO NOT TOUCH group because they bite and it is very painful.

This one was on the railing of the stairs at work. He kind of danced as he walked. It was really cute.

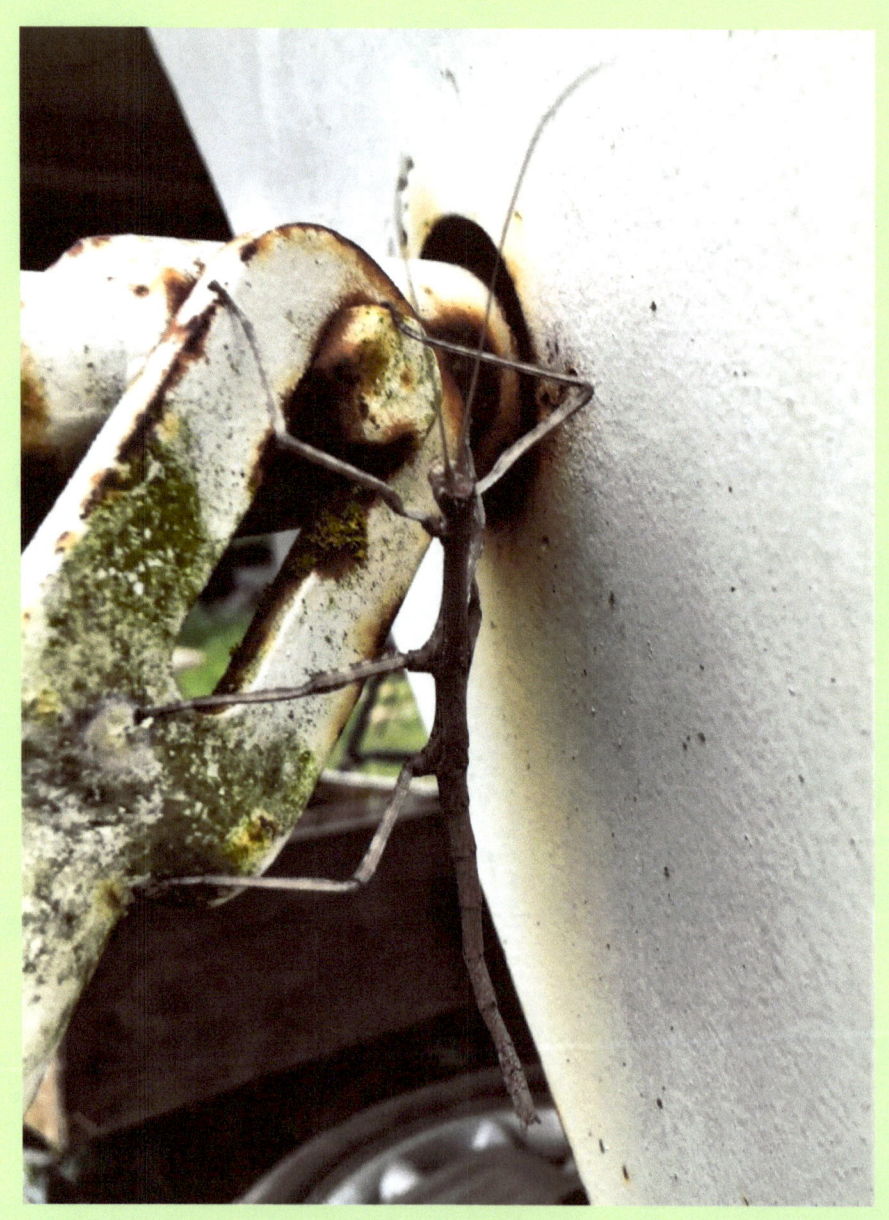

Stick bug – gray

They can regrow their legs to escape being eaten. They sway when they walk to act like a stick in the wind. They hide the evidence of their growing by eating the shed exoskeleton.

This guy was on the trailer hitch to the horse trailer. He hides well.

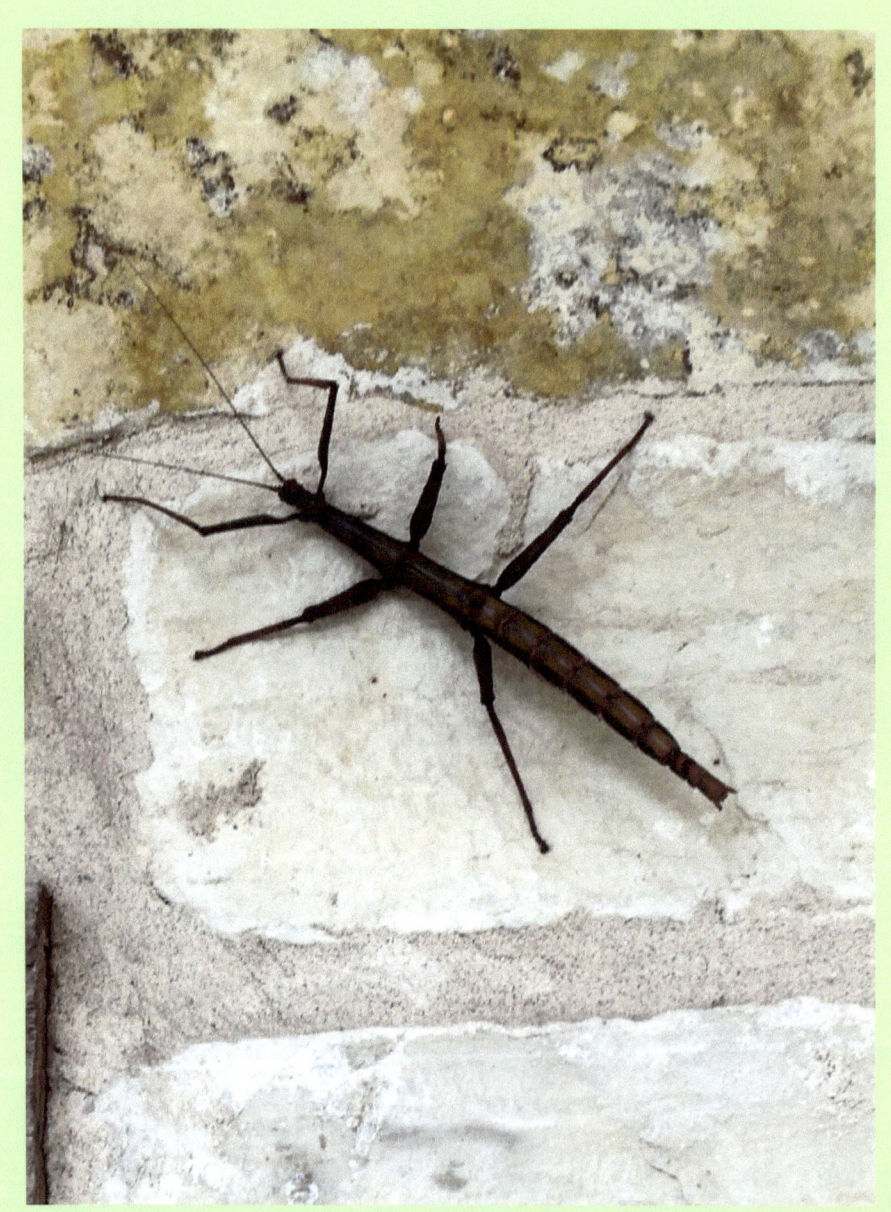

Stick bug – colorful

They do not bite, but their legs have spikes on them. So, picking them up can be like picking up a cactus. They can fake bleed from the many joints in their body. And they can spray a foul chemical like tear gas to keep predators away.

This colorful guy was on the wall by the door to the house.

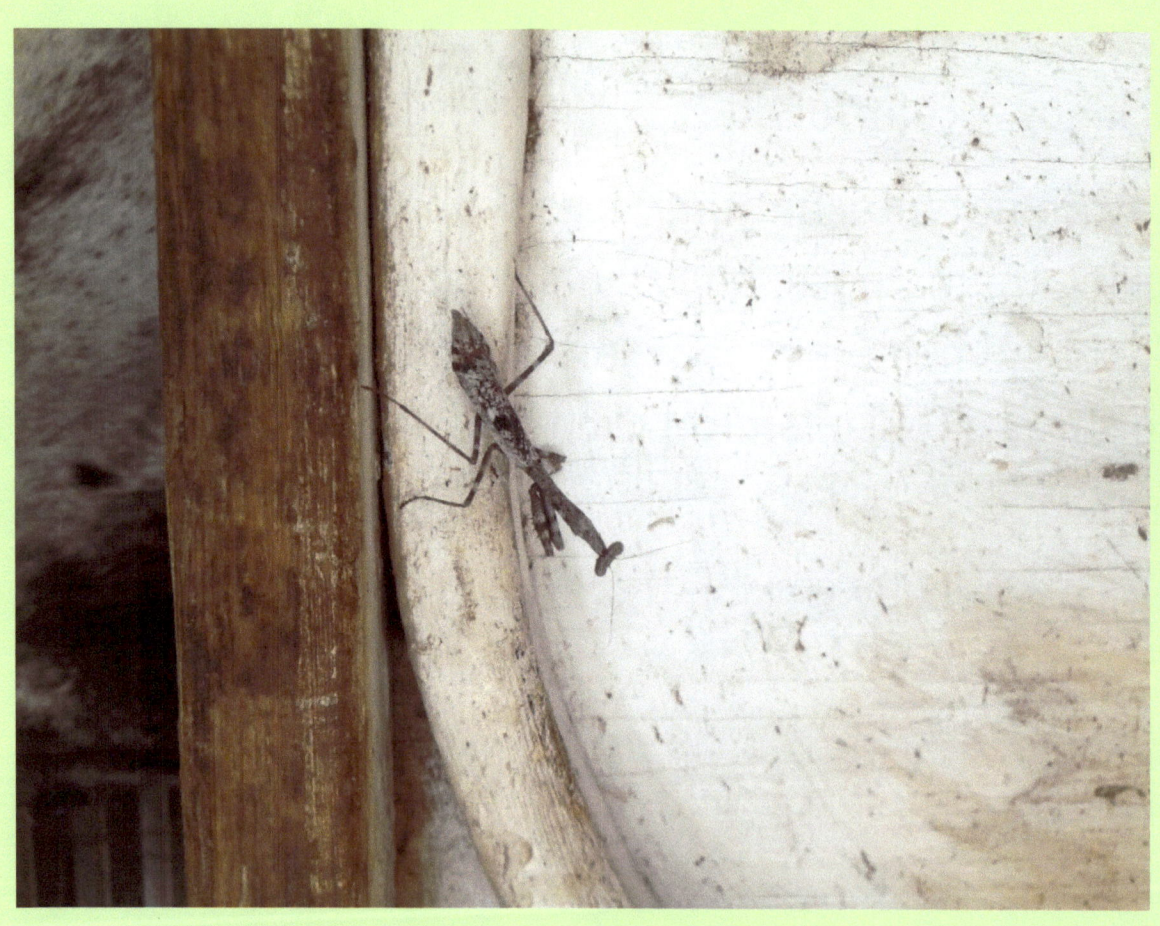

Praying Mantis – Adult, gray

Adults can be 1 to 16 cm long. They eat bugs and are really good for the garden. And they can even be pets.

Mike and Mason wanted to keep him.

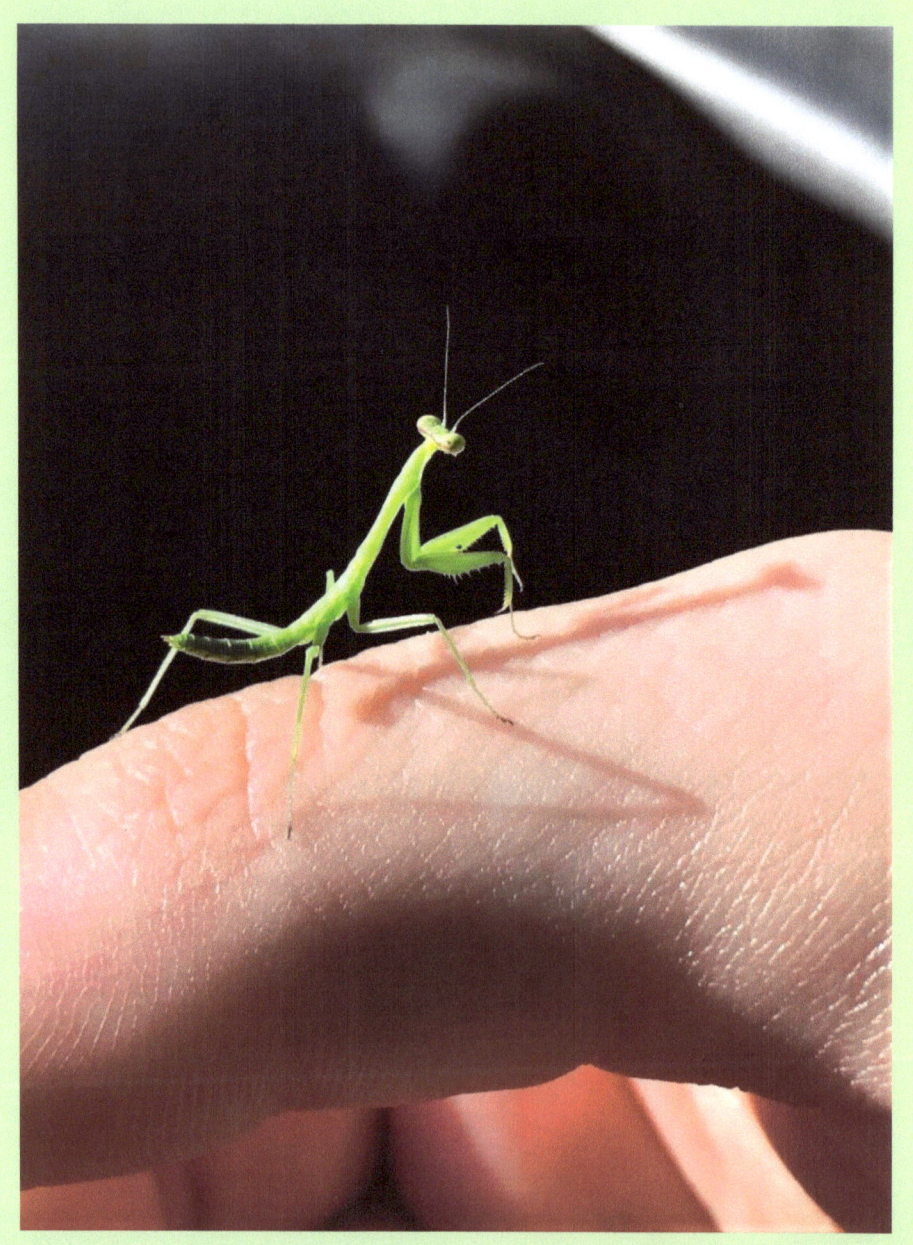

Praying mantis – green, baby on a finger

They can turn their heads 180 degrees – a whole half circle.

The very long front legs have rows of sharp spines to help them hold their food. They bend those legs when they move about making them look like they are praying.

This guy was in my car and was dancing to the music.

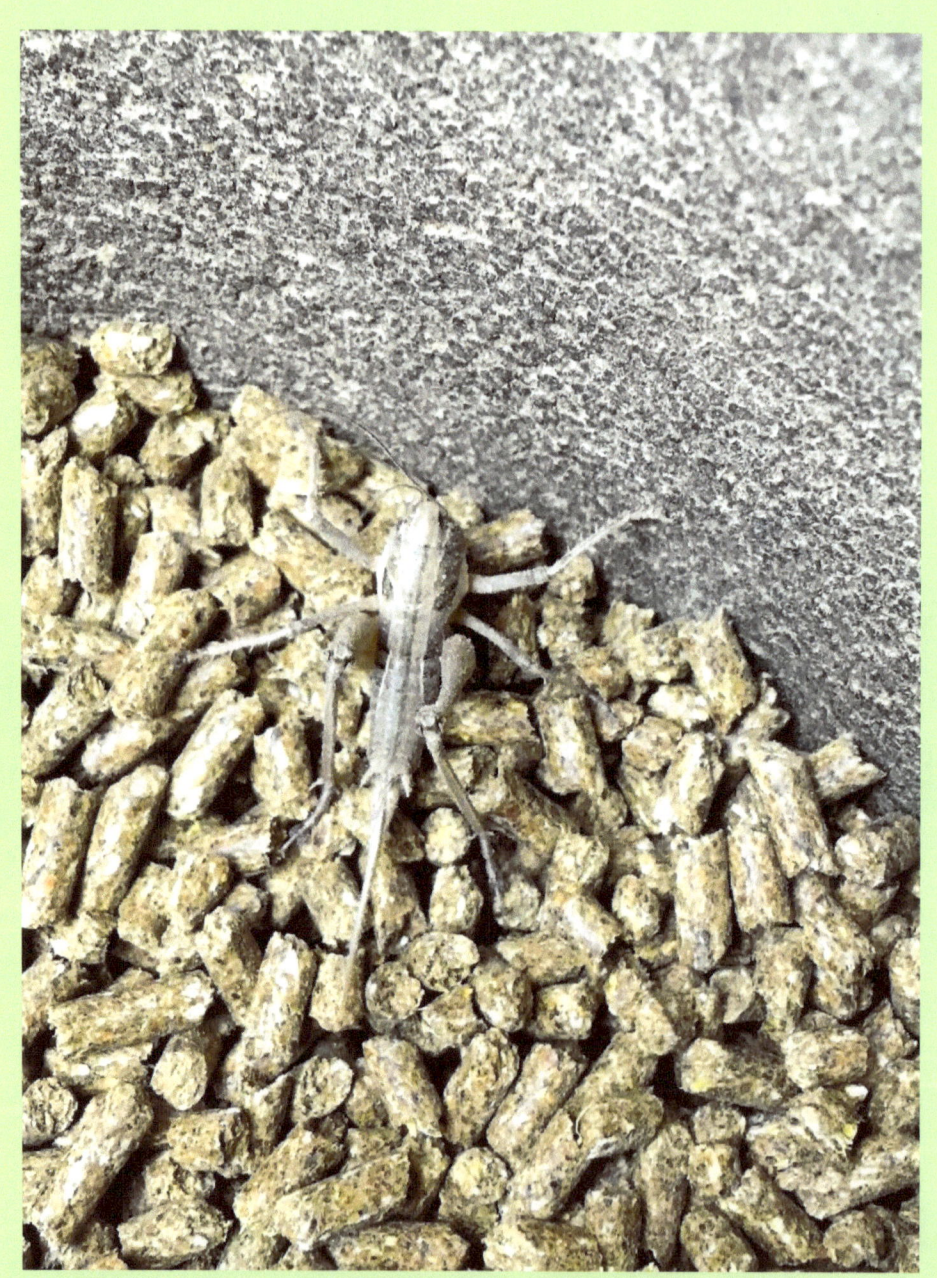

Oak Bush Cricket

Or Katydid, Or long-horned grasshopper.

They eat lots of leaves and destroy trees. They have lots of colors and sizes.

Found in a bucket of horse feed. Blends in so well I almost missed it.

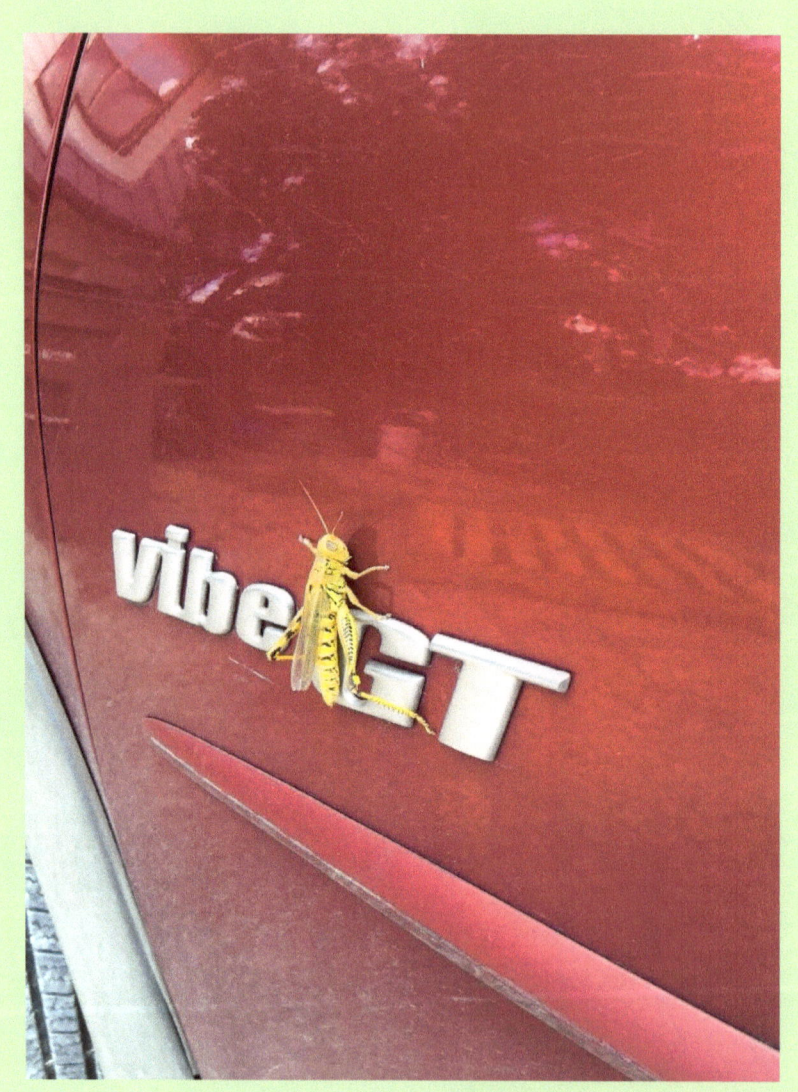

Differential Grasshopper

Adults can be as big as two inches long. They have very strong wings and have been seen by airplane pilots as high as 1400 feet in the air.

They are pests and eat all the corn and wheat crops.

This one was on my car and the sound he made was very loud. I thought it was a wounded hummingbird.

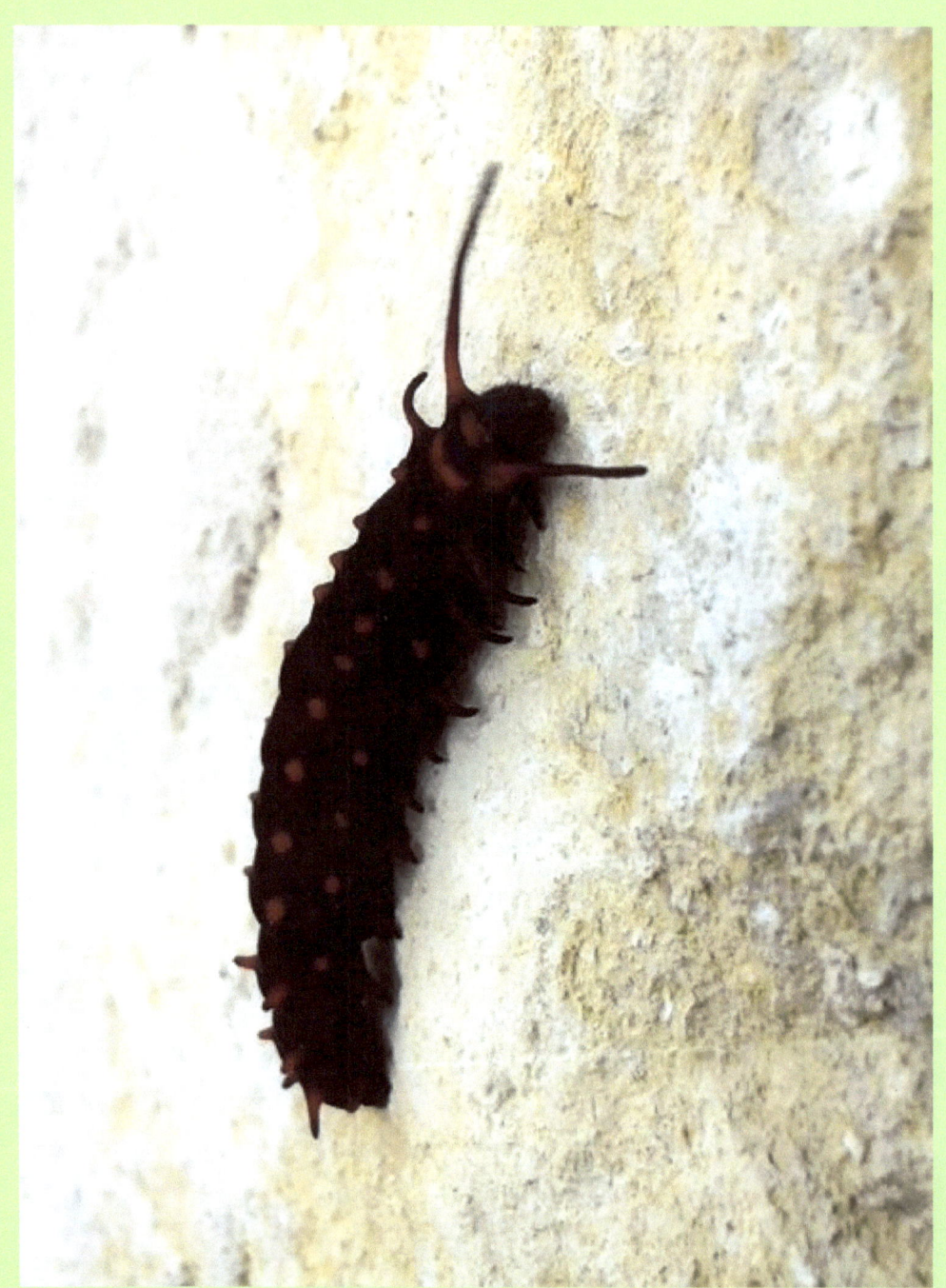

Pipevine Swallowtail Caterpillar crawling up the outside wall of my house. They turn into a beautiful florescent blue butterfly.

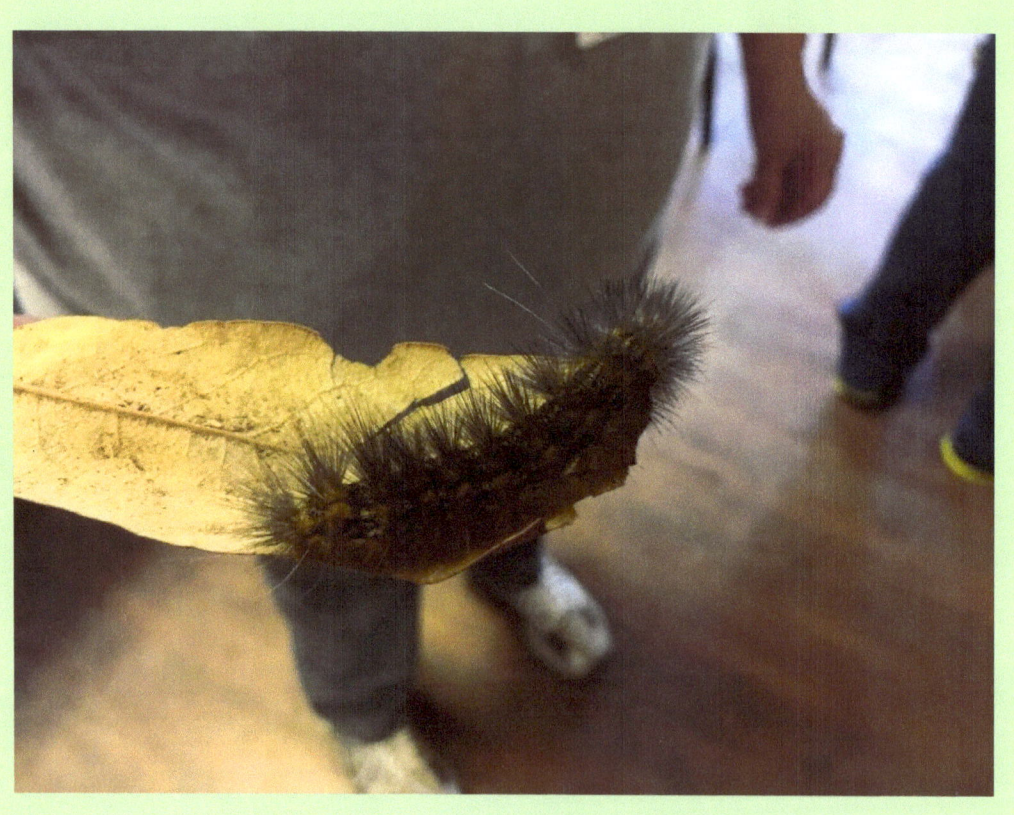

Saltmarsh Caterpillar

These caterpillars can be found across the United States and not always in marsh land. They eat lots of leaves before using their hairy spines to create cocoons. They hatch after only two weeks in the cocoon and become the Acrea moth.

This one was found at the Barn by one of the riders who brought it in to show us how big it was.

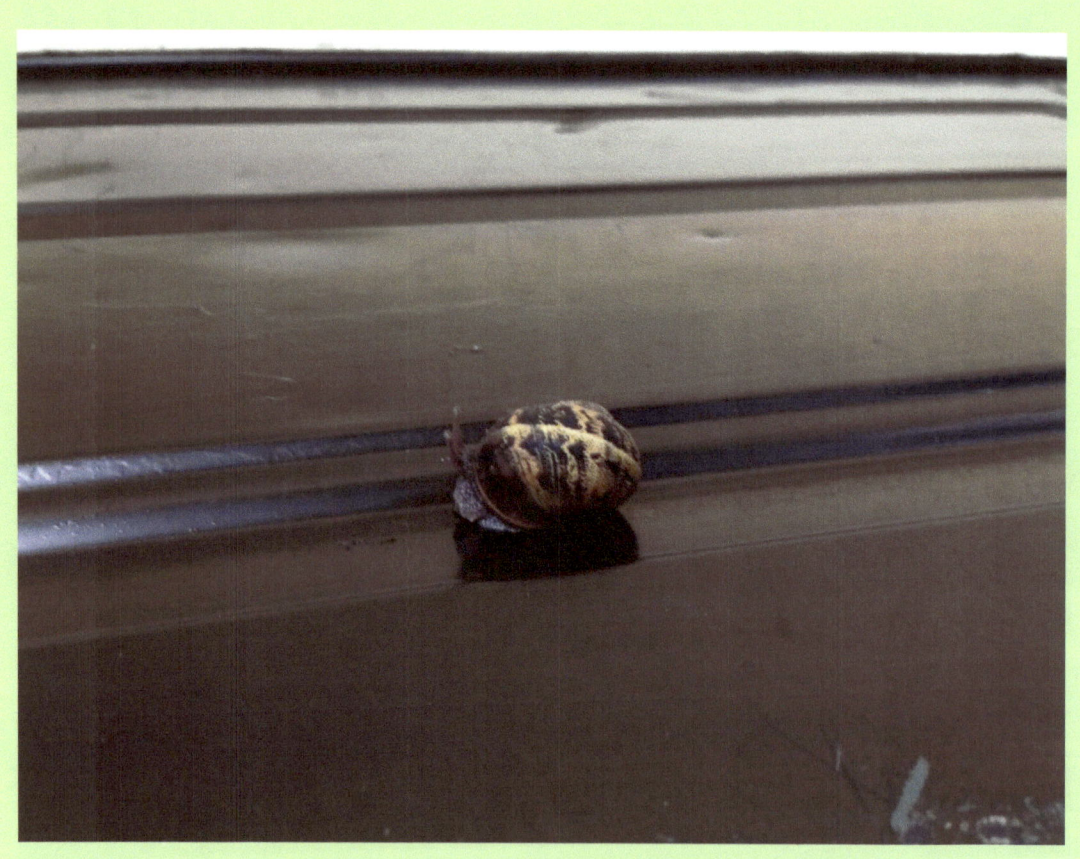

Garden Snail

You can tell a snails age by how many rings it has. This one is real young because it only has the half circle shell so far.

This one was crawling up the door of the house.

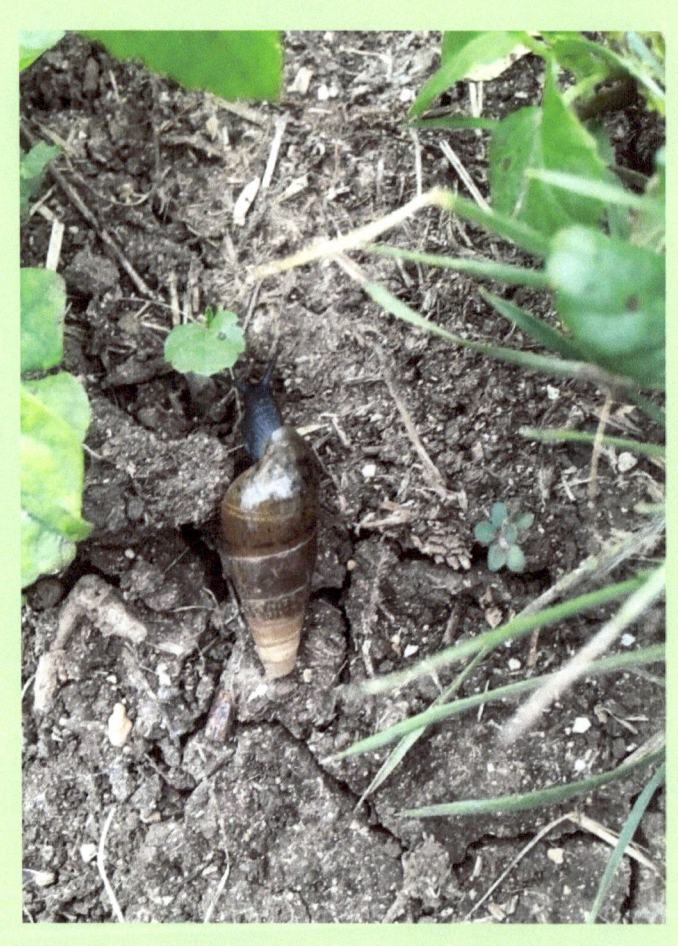

Decollate Snail

First introduced to eat the land snail, it has now become a pest to areas where the land snail is not available.

It is an omnivore. It eats both plants and animals like bugs and other small snails.

I found this one crawling in the pasture near the fence.

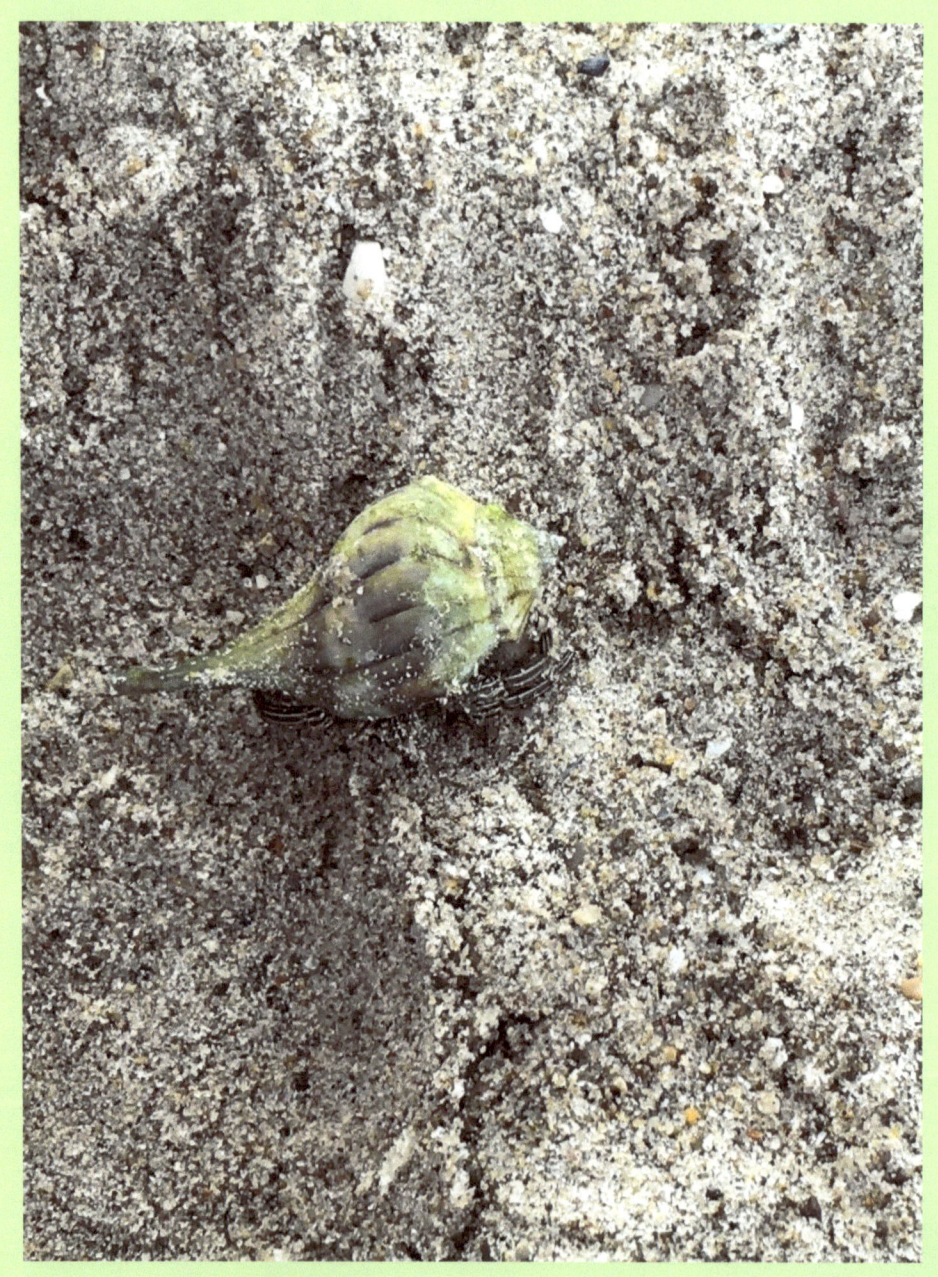

Marine Hermit crab –

They live in the ocean and can grow from 2 – 8 inches long. They have lots of different colors on shells and bodies.

When it gets too big for its shell he will go in search of a new one. It will only take a shell that is empty.

Mason and Mike stepped on him while swimming in the Gulf Coast off Corpus Christi.

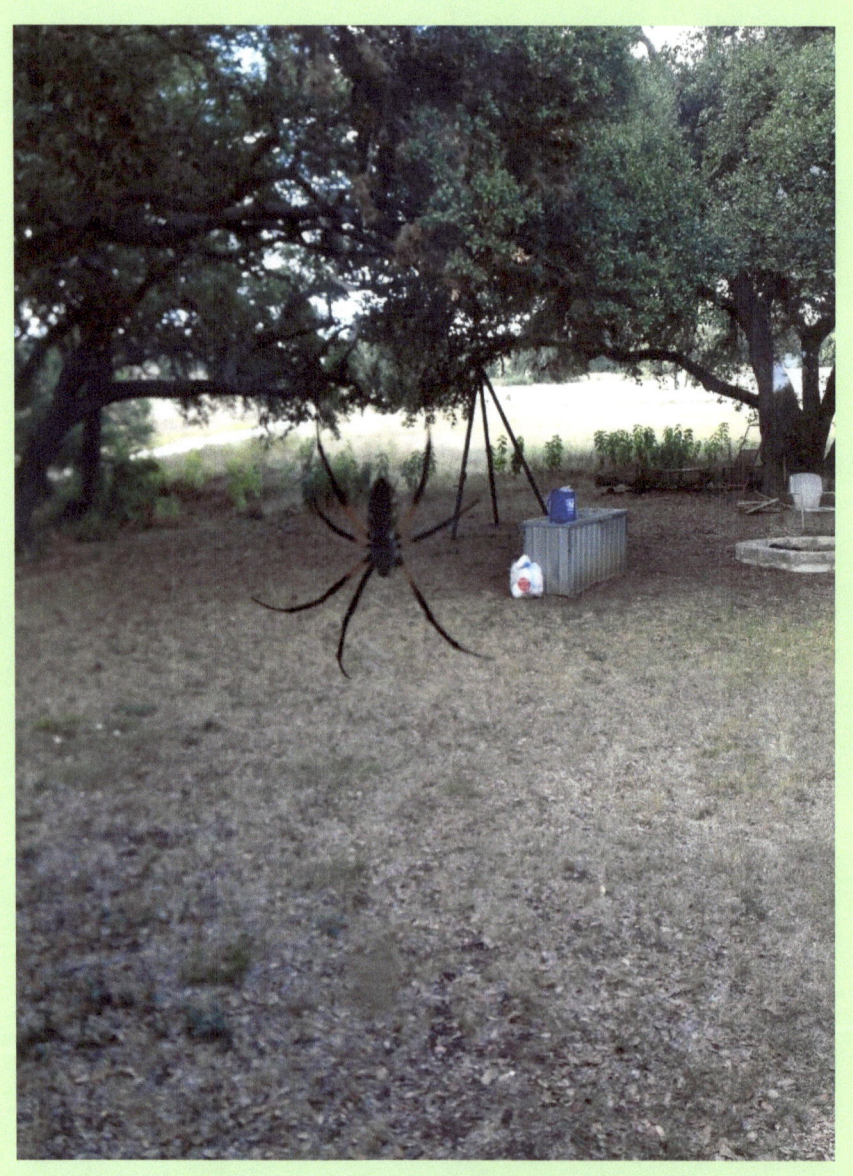

Garden spider – also an orb weaver.

Garden spiders have poor eyesight and rely on their great sense of vibrations to locate the food caught in the web.

The web usually has a zigzag down the middle of the web. Spiders hang with head pointing to the ground.

She's black and orange and hangs out in the shade of the rooftops of houses.

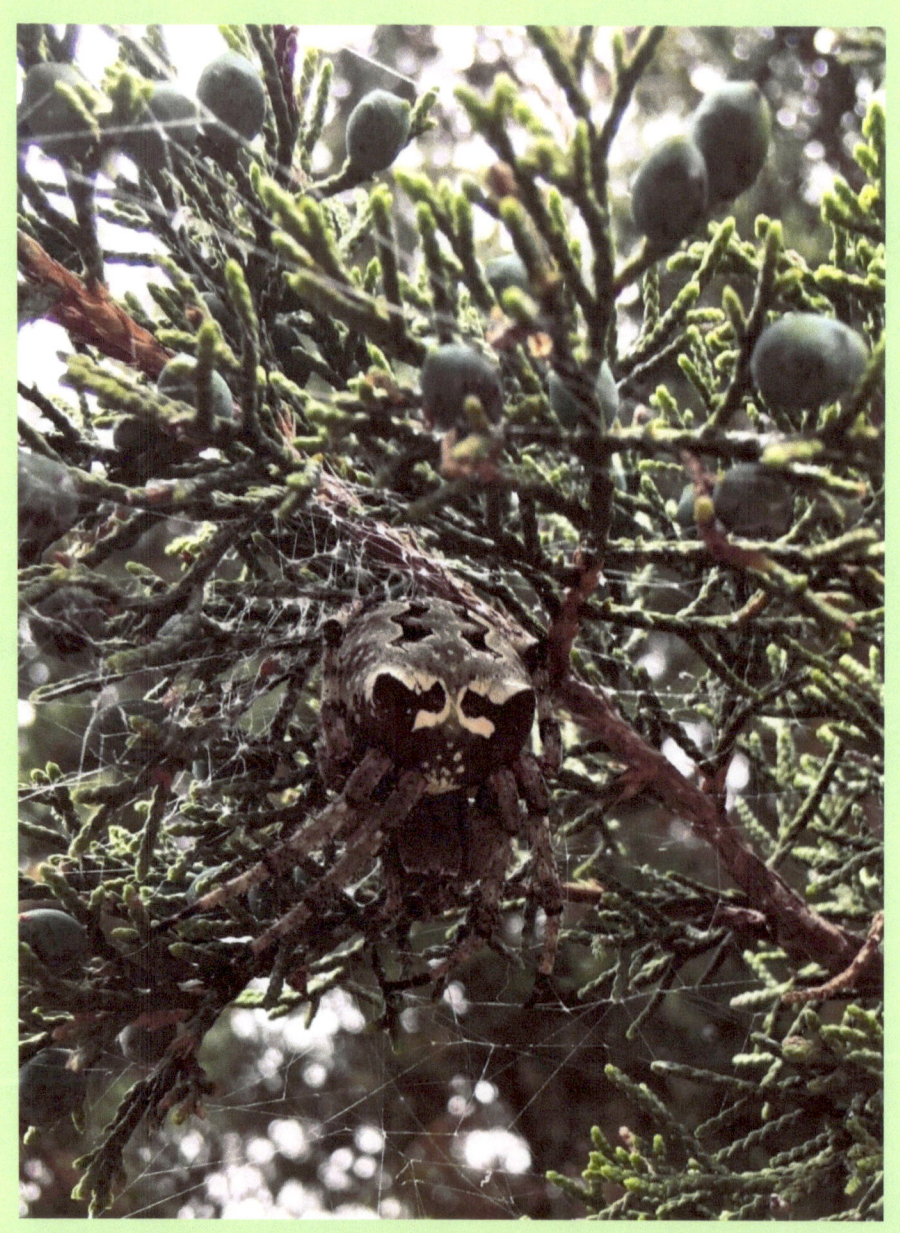

Giant Lichen Orb Weaver

The web is 6-8 feet in diameter and her body is half the size of a golf ball.

They hide in the corner of the web under a branch to not be eaten by birds. They come out of hiding at night.

I walked into three of these walking to work one morning. They love the Hemlock trees.

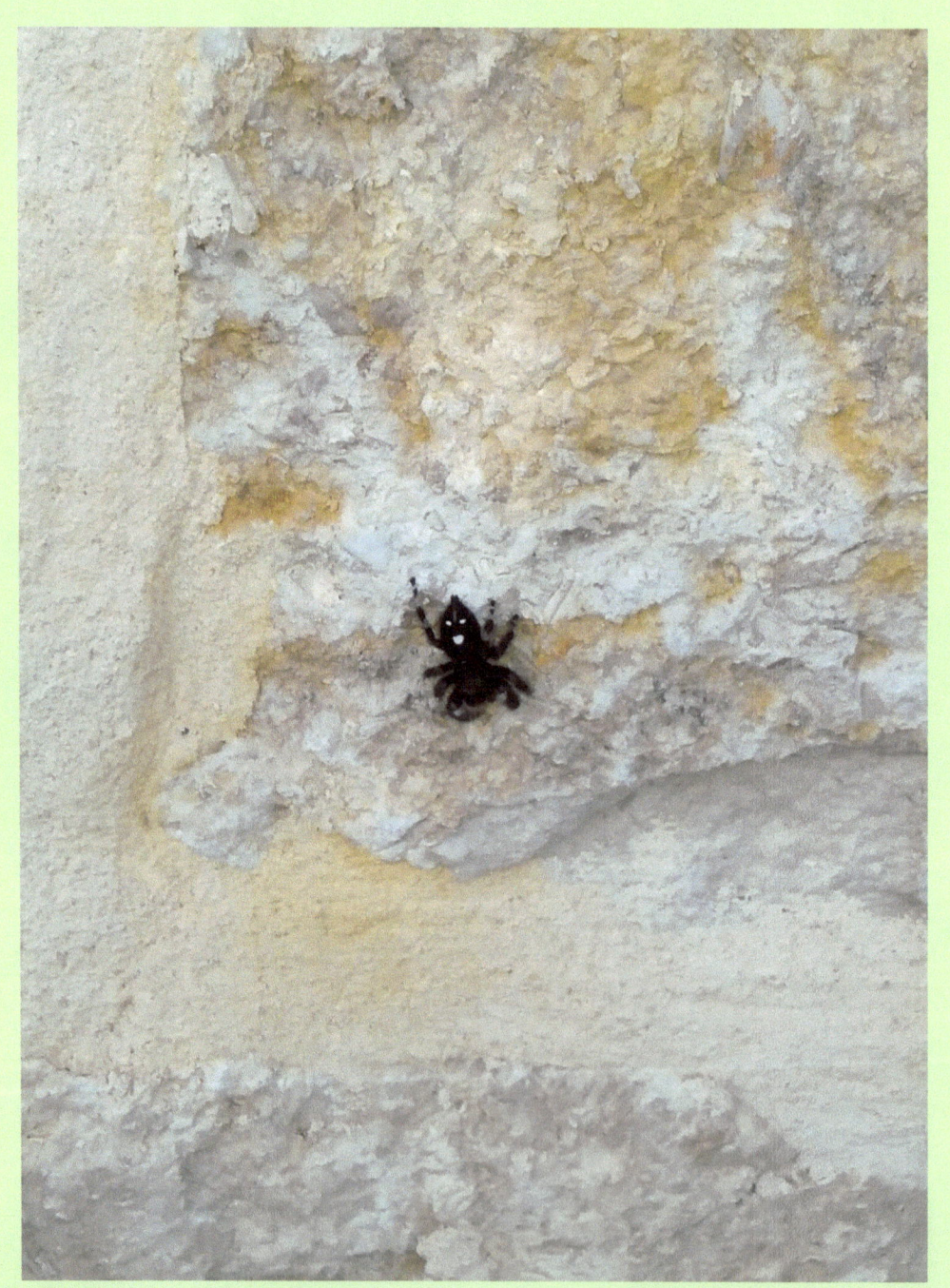

The Bold Jumping Spider

They don't make webs they jump.

We call them the ghost spiders cause all you can see sometimes is their white spots that look like eyes and mouth.

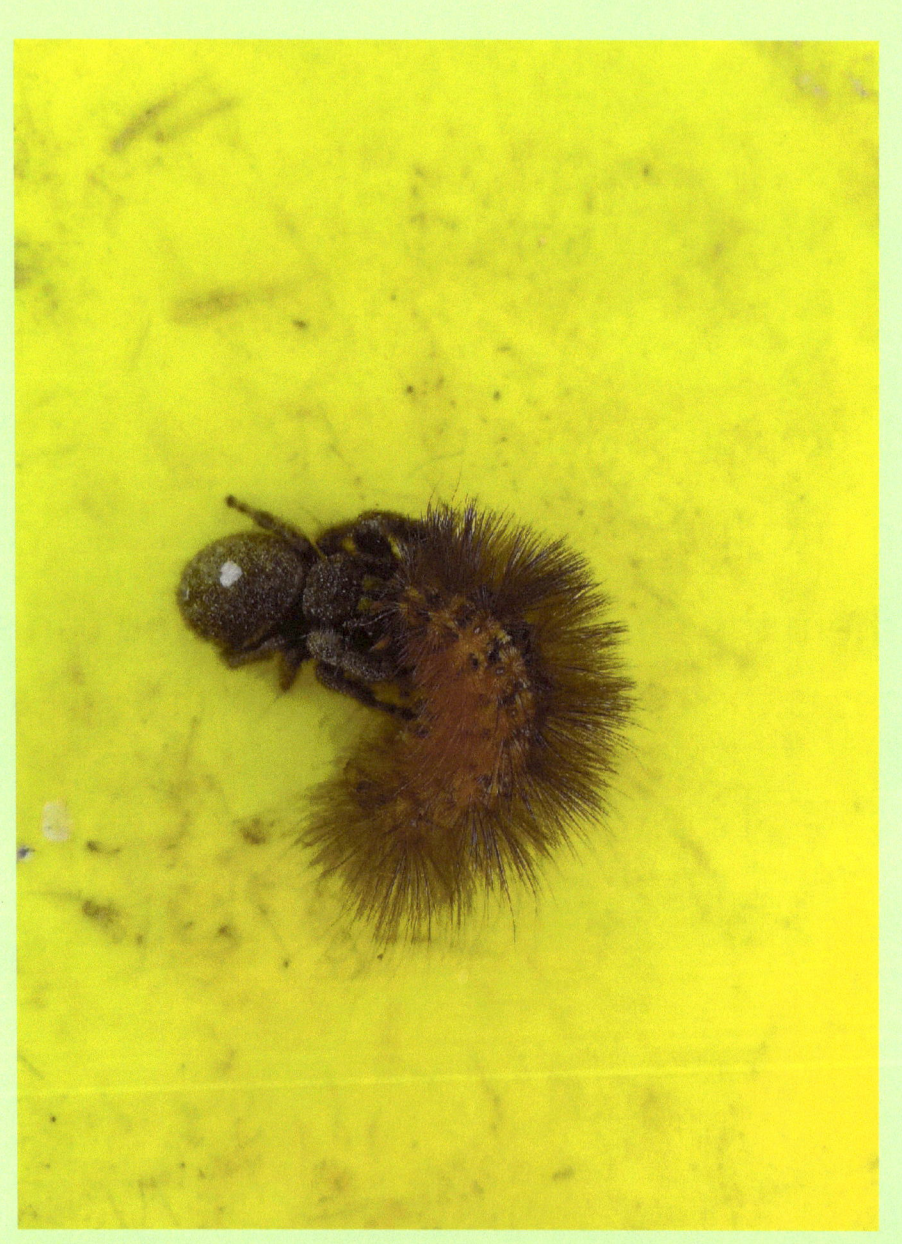

This Bold Jumping spider is eating a caterpillar, the not so nice kind that eats my garden plants. Good spider.

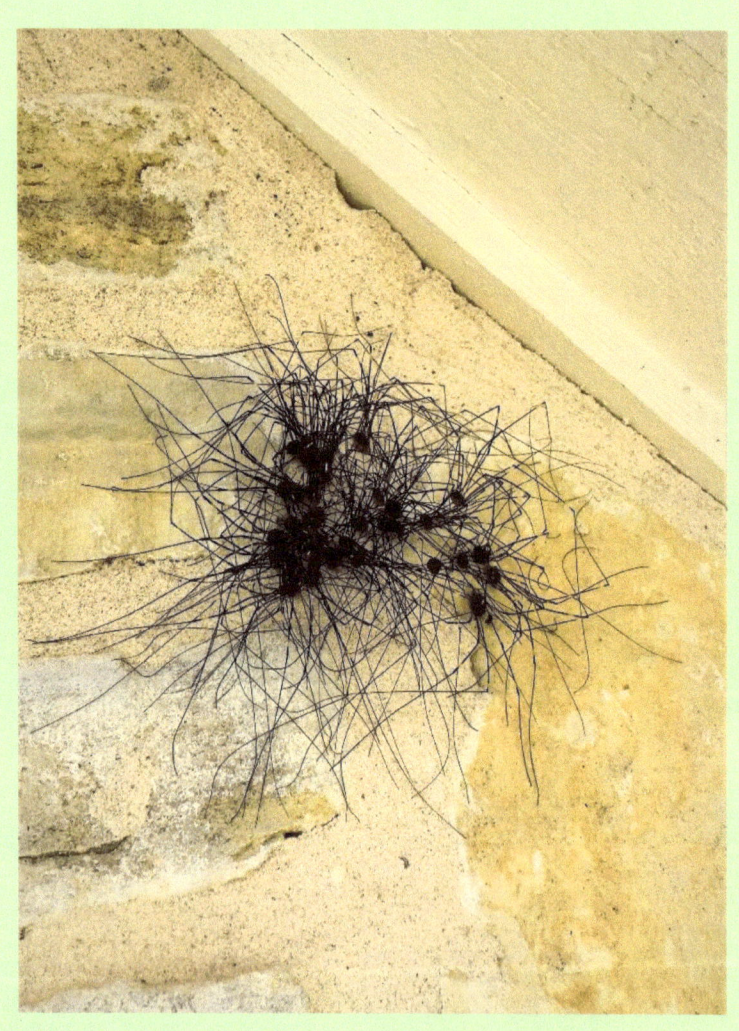

Daddy Long Legs

The pulsing Daddy Longlegs. They gather in the heat of the day and bounce together. It's because they sleep during the day and can't make webs to get away from predators and they have a smelly odor that is multiplied when together.

This group hangs out at the top of my house just under the eaves.

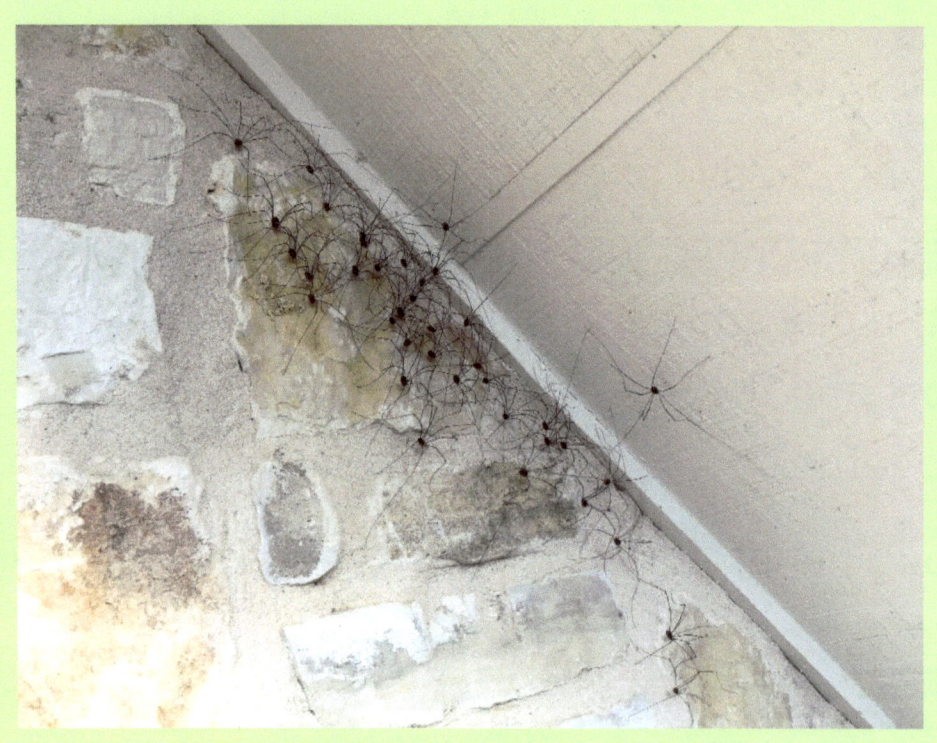

The gathering.

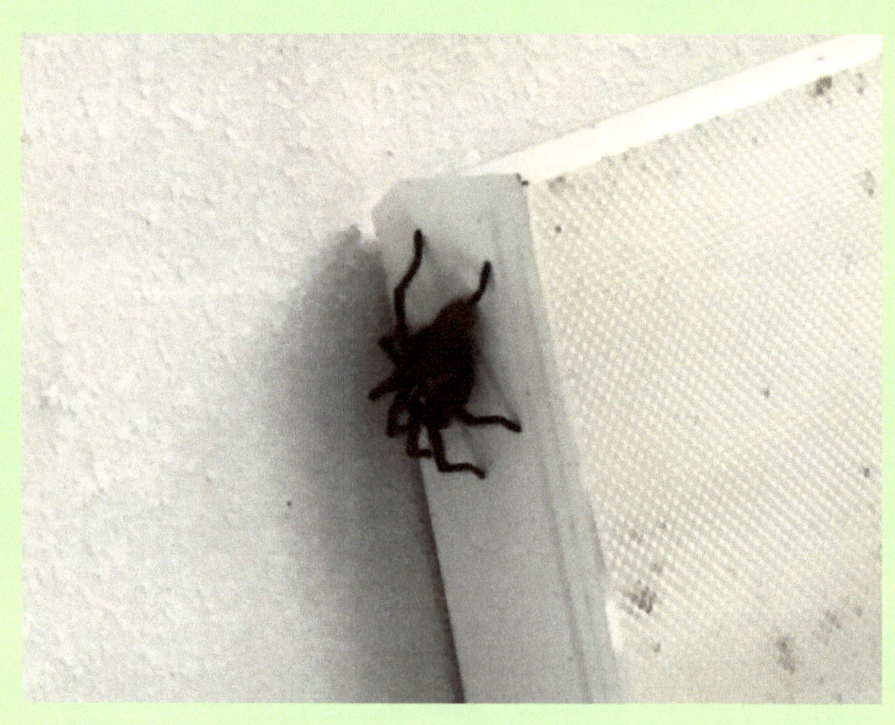

Tarantula

Big hairy spiders. They do not weave a web but will spin a "trip-wire" to protect them from predators.

They have painful bites but their venom is weaker than a bee sting.

During molting, they replace their outer exoskeleton and inner organs like stomach lining and can regrow legs.

This one lives in our garage and Mike named him Aragog.

NO TOUCH BUGS

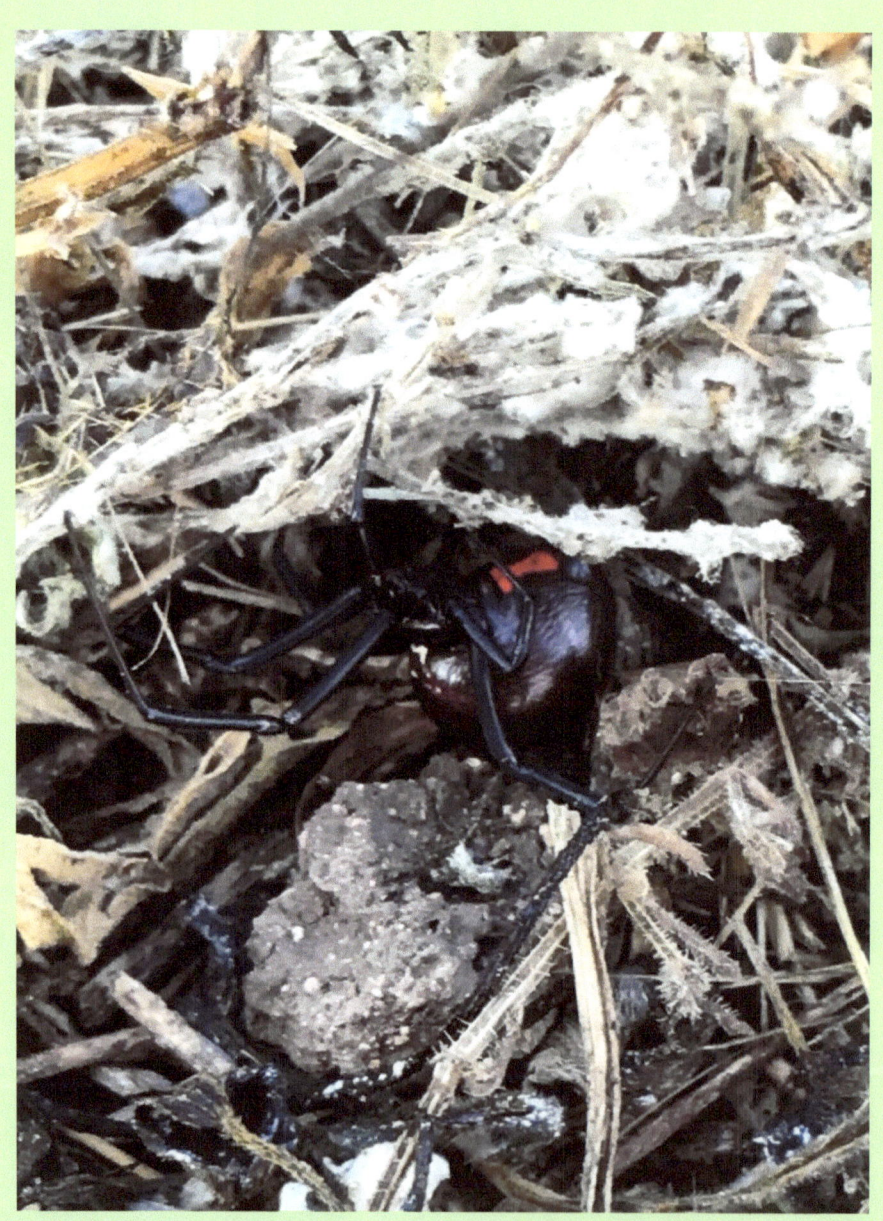

Black Widow Spider – Very Poisonous and Very Deadly

Their venom is 15 times stronger than a rattlesnake.

Only females have the red hourglass mark on their belly. And eats her husband after mating.

She was found under the water tank in the pasture with the horses. Mike and Mason removed her to a safe place in the woods.

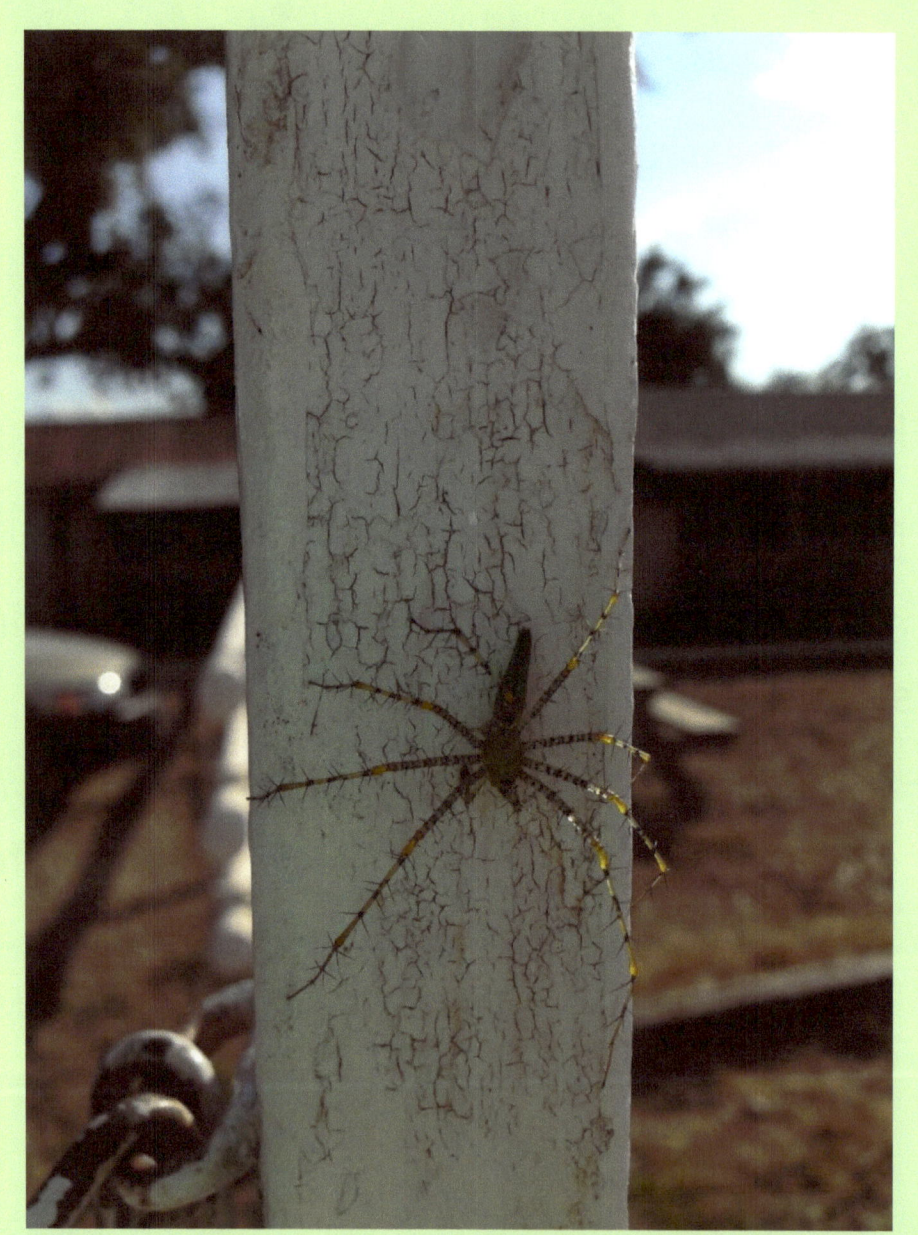

Green Lynx Spider.

This interesting little guy was on the gate post to the pasture where the horses graze.

Also goes with the NO TOUCH bugs. Its bite is poisonous but not deadly; leaves a 7 – 10" red swelling at site of bite.

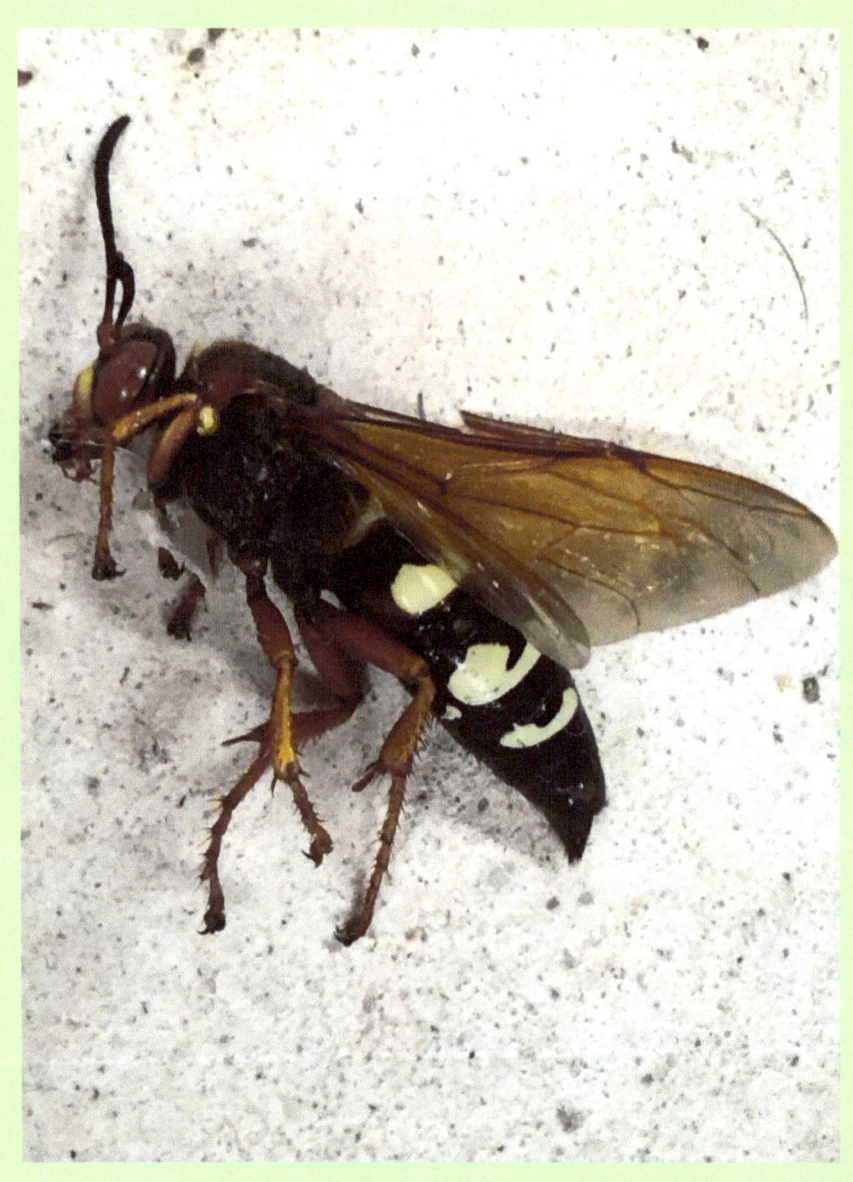

Cicada Killer Wasp/Giant ground hornets –

The females sting but the males don't. It's a big ouch but not poisonous. They live in the ground during the winter and come out in the spring to pollenate the flowers.

This one was flying around inside our garage. It almost flew into my hair. Thanks to Mason I did not get stung.

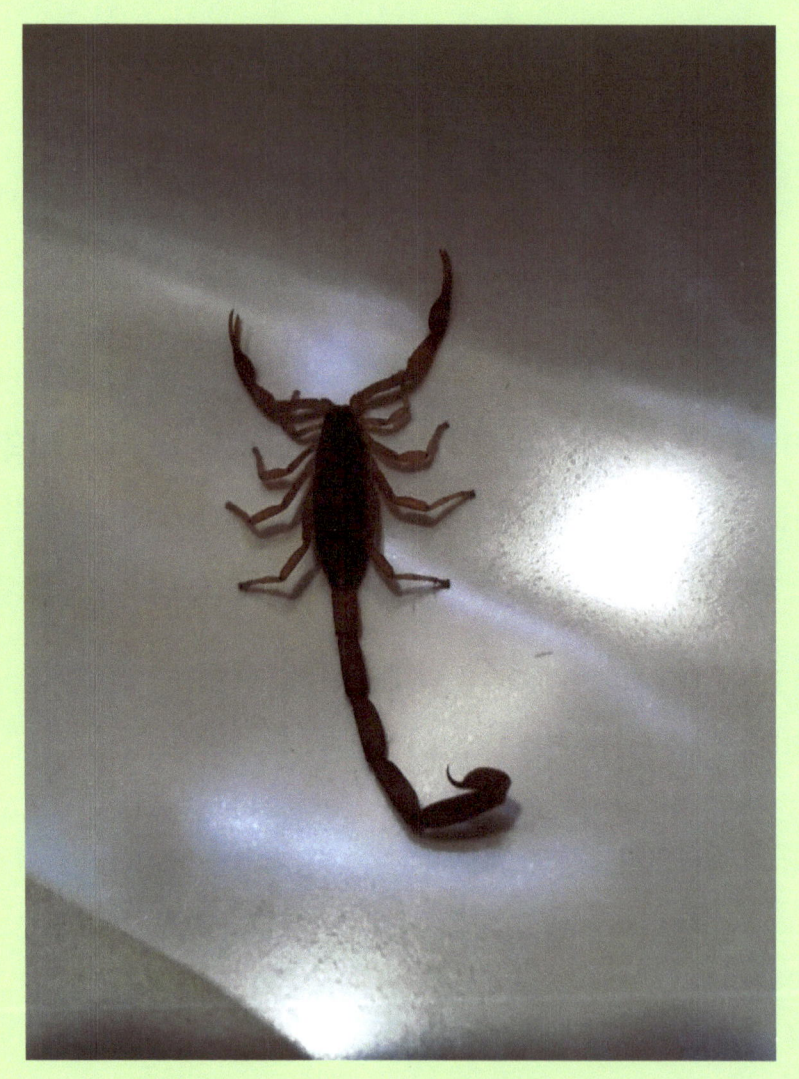

Striped Bark Scorpion

The stings are not poisonous but hurt a lot.

Adults are about 2 and ¼ inches long. They like to live under rocks and in dead trees. They can live to be 20-25 years old and can have several "broods" in one year which are carried on the back of the mommy scorpion.

This wonderful guy was found in my bathtub. I am glad I looked before I stepped in.

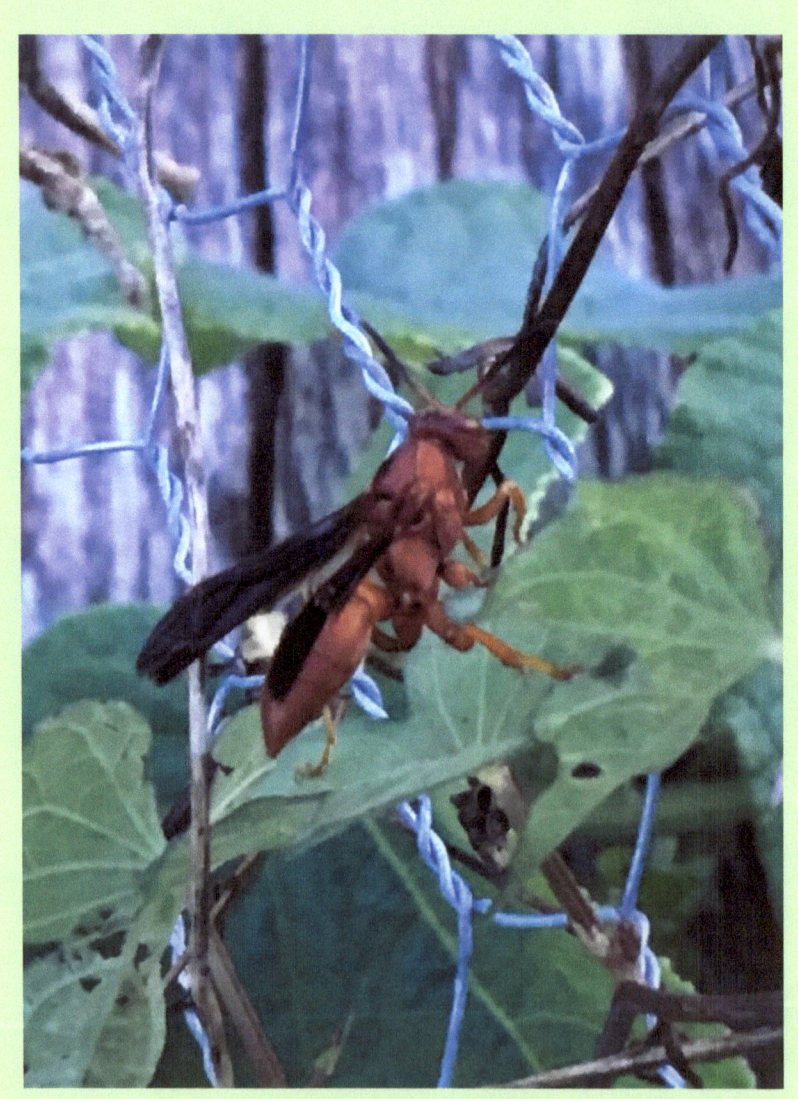

Red Wasps

Females are the ones that sting when they are protecting the nest.

This is what I got stung by and went to the hospital because I was allergic. I stay away from them now.

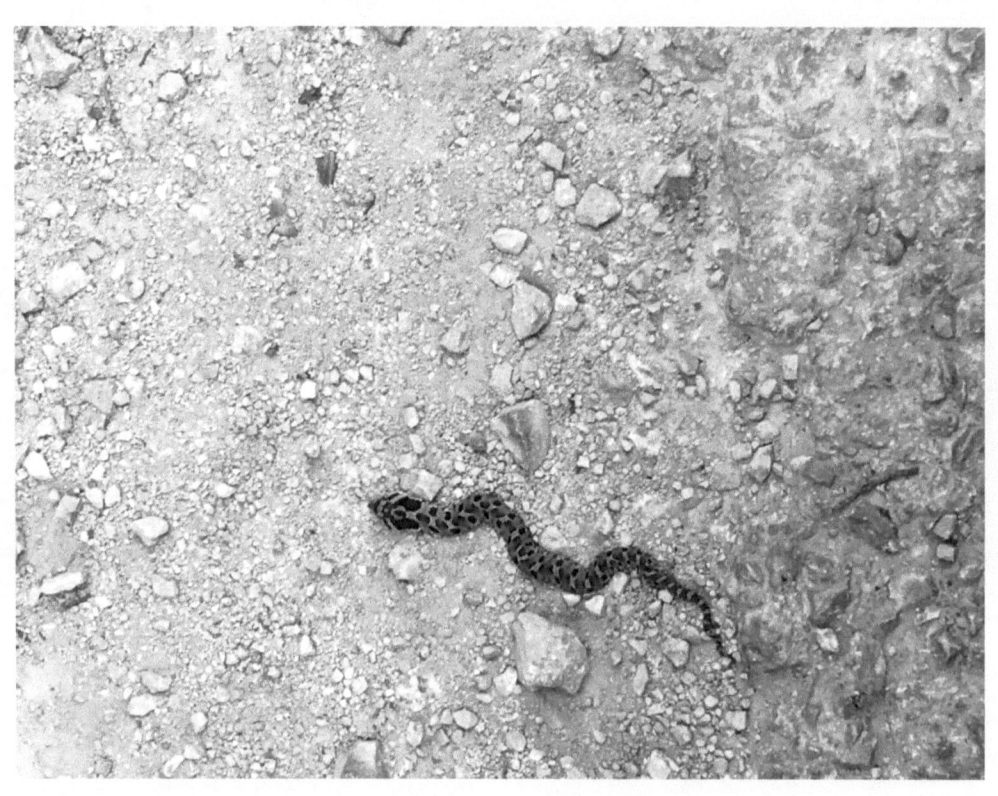

Hognose snake.

Not poisonous.

Flattens out to play dead. When it does strike it does not bite but hits with its heavily keeled snout.

It grows to about 3 feet when adult and can live up to 18 years.

This one crawled across the driveway on my way to work. It is very small and flattened out laying very still until after I had moved past it.

Happy bug hunting Reigan.

I hope that you forever keep your great enthusiasm for the creepy crawly things in the world around us.